Heartfelt Hymns for All Seasons

Inspired music for worship

Shelly Hamilton

Edited and Engraved by Alan Lohr
Cover Design by Patti Jeffers

ISBN: 978-0-7877-1146-7

©2015 SoundForth
Distributed by The Lorenz Corporation,
P.O. Box 802, Dayton, OH 45401-0802
800-444-1144 · www.lorenz.com

Foreword

Webster tells us that a hymn is a song of praise to God. I don't know of a better way to lift your spirits than by praising God through hymns. Music has been a part of my life about as long as my memory has. I am deeply thankful for God's gift of music and I am also thankful for the blessing of giving that gift back to Him!

There are many "seasons" in a Christian's life—there are seasons we mark on a calendar. Every Christmas and Easter we sing hymns to celebrate the life and death of our Savior. There are also "seasons" we go through over the span of our lives. There are seasons of great joy when we celebrate the beginning of a precious life; seasons of incredible sorrow when we say goodbye to those we love; seasons of blessing; seasons of deep trial. God equipped us with music and musicianship to praise Him in every season!

My desire is that *Heartfelt Hymns for All Seasons* will be a blessing to you as you bless the Lord through every season of your life!

"The just shall live by faith."

—Shelly Hamilton

Contents

I Love to Tell the Story

HANKEY

William G. Fischer
Arranged by SHELLY HAMILTON

www.lorenz.com

6

Come, Thou Fount of Every Blessing

NETTLETON

John Wyeth
Arranged by SHELLY HAMILTON

www.lorenz.com

Dedicated to my beloved son, Jonathan Campbell Hamilton, 1979-2013

When We All Get to Heaven

HEAVEN

Emily D. Wilson
Arranged by SHELLY HAMILTON

www.lorenz.com

My Jesus, I Love Thee

GORDON

Adoniram J. Gordon
Arranged by SHELLY HAMILTON

Slowly and meditatively ♩ = 66

www.lorenz.com

Like a River Glorious

WYE VALLEY

James Mountain
Arranged by SHELLY HAMILTON

Flowing ♩. = 76

www.lorenz.com

Battle Hymn of the Republic

BATTLE HYMN

Traditional American melody
Arranged by SHELLY HAMILTON

www.lorenz.com

Christ Arose

CHRIST AROSE

Robert Lowry
Arranged by SHELLY HAMILTON

 www.lorenz.com

Joy to the World

ANTIOCH

George Frederick Handel
Arranged by SHELLY HAMILTON